THE MYSTERIOUS MAGI OF CHRISTMAS

RENEWING THE CHRISTMAS MYSTIQUE BY DISTINGUISHING THE BIBLICAL FROM THE TRADITIONAL

Mike Brown

Second Edition
Written by Mike Brown

Published by OneHope Publishing
Printed by Kendell Direct, an Amazon.com Company
Available from Amazon.com, Kendell Direct.com, and other retail outlets

Heartfelt appreciation is expressed to Cheryl Brown, Shirley Penick, and Sherrie Davidson for their significant support in proofreading and editing of this book. Also to Jim Stevenson whose review has led to this second edition.

Cover design: Berge Design

Scripture Copyright Permissions:
Scripture quotations marked (ESV) are taken from the ESV® Bible (The Holy Bible, English Standard Version®), copyright © 2001 by Crossway, a publishing ministry of Good News Publishers. Used by permission. All rights reserved."

Scripture quotations marked (NKJV) are taken from the New King James Version®. Copyright © 1982 by Thomas Nelson. Used by permission. All rights reserved.

Scripture quotations marked (NIV) are taken from the Holy Bible, New International Version®, NIV®. Copyright © 1973, 1978, 1984, 2011 by Biblica, Inc.™ Used by permission of Zondervan. All rights reserved worldwide.

Old Testament dates and time intervals taken from Thompson Chain Reference Bible, New International Version, Copyright © 1983 by The B. B. Kirkbride Bible Company, Inc. and The Zondervan Corporation

Copyright© 2016 - Mike Brown
Copyright© Second Edition 2023 Mike Brown

All rights reserved under International Copyright Law. Permission is granted to copy exerts from this book for non-profit usage, so long as such copy does not violate scripture copyrights.

ISBN 978-0-9976300-1-5

Other Books by this Author:

- ❖ Celebrating God's Purpose for the Ages
  Drawing Nearer to the God of Origin and Eternal Destiny Through Bible Prophecy (2016 paperback 450 pages, available on Amazon. ISBN 978-0-9976300-0-8)

- ❖ The Vision of the Patriarchs
  Messages to Us from Revealed Insights of the Hebrew Pioneers (2016 paperback 60 pages, available on Amazon. ISBN 978-0-9976300-2-2)

- ❖ Something to Boast About
  Uncovering and Meeting Every Person's Greatest Need of the Heart (2018 paperback 55 pages, available on Amazon. ISBN 978-0-9976300-3-9)

- ❖ When God Answers
  Like Memorial Stones, Answered Prayer Testifies that God is Listening (2019 paperback 90 pages, available on Amazon. ISBN 978-0-9976300-5-3)

- ❖ Treasuring the Season
  An organizer, devotional and printable source for guiding Christmas anticipation and joy amidst a hectic holiday culture. Co-authored with principal author and daughter Leanne Phelps (2019 paperback 100 pages, available on Amazon. ISBN 978-0-9976300-4-6)

- ❖ Mysteries Concealed or Truth Revealed?
  Exploring the Parables of Jesus (2020 paperback 405 pages, available on Amazon. ISBN 978-0-9976300-6-0)

- ❖ The Substitute
  A Message to Us from Barabbas (2022 paperback 40 pages, available on Amazon. ISBN 978-0-9976300-7-7)

Conventions

In order to make this study as readable as possible, scripture text is included in the book text. Scriptural quotations are indented and italicized to clearly identify them, like this:

> *Matthew 13:16 (NKJV)*
> *[16] "But blessed are your eyes for they see, and your ears for they hear; [17] for assuredly, I say to you that many prophets and righteous men desired to see what you see, and did not see it, and to hear what you hear, and did not hear it.*

Scripture quoted as part of the commentary text is italicized without quotation marks, like this: 'Other groups of the king's advisors are the *magicians* who . . .'

Contents

Chapter	Page
1. The Magic of Christmas	1
2. Who Were These Wise Men?	5
3. The Journey of the Magi	11
4. Prophecy in Their Heads	15
5. The Magi Encounter Jerusalem	23
6. The Star	27
7. The Magi Worship	37
8. Reflecting	45

Chapter 1

The Magic of Christmas

For many of us, Christmas is a time which evokes joyful memories and implements long-standing traditions. So it was with me. Christmas was my most over-the-top holiday. As a child, I often got so excited in anticipation that I nearly made myself sick and had to lay down for a bit. Of course, my excitement was all about the opening of gifts, set within the magical fantasy of the season. I was infatuated by the whole experience. Our family made a big deal of the preparation and family fellowship. We gathered with both sides of the family in multiple celebrations. Our gatherings were very predictable and soon became tradition. It was my favorite time of year, and now my wife and two daughters and their families would echo that sentiment. We love Christmas.

As I moved from childhood to being a teenager, I remember still loving the Christmas experience, but I was also quite aware that the magic was fading. There was a period when I remember being consciously a little sorrowful at its leaving. I still loved Christmas with its activities, and was happy with the holidays, but it was the mystique that I missed. I remember assuming it must be just an inevitable relic of growing up, but I still missed it. This mindset took me into young adulthood.

Then I met Cheryl, and I began going to her church, and we married. Shortly, a very pivotal thing happened. Because of her dynamic faith, and my changed culture of worship, I opened my mind and heart to the Lord and began walking in his truth. Change began. Let me interject that I grew up going to church, knowing about and believing in the Lord of the Bible, but now a light was coming on. Until then, I was living in an inherited faith. Now, with Cheryl's influence, I began to take my faith personally and seriously. That was my time of first experiencing tangible regeneration. One change that occurred was I distinctly remember the mystique was back in Christmas, almost as if I were a child again. As I learned to love the scriptures, I found myself getting excited about the 'magic' of Christmas again. This brings me up to the present time.

Of course, this new mystique was not the anticipation of opening gifts, great food and family fellowship, although we enjoyed all those festivities and still do. It was the joyful awareness of the working of God in history to redeem us, revealing Himself in the nativity stories. It was the realization that all of this was part of a grand master-plan in the mind of God. It was the ancient predictions of prophets, now made history. It was the myriad of unanswered questions. The 'magic' was back because now I more clearly saw the God who was involved in it.

Traditions
We have this insatiable knack for being attracted by the superficial rather than the real. We allow meaningful things to be supplanted with familiar, comfortable things. Things that once had meaning, we still do, but the meaning has faded. The thing itself becomes the focus. Traditions are not bad, but they can be dangerous to our growing in Christ. Christmas, like so many things we practice, has become a victim of much tradition. Some of what we celebrate is biblical, but some of it seems to be assumed, or worse, motivated by materialistic initiative. Any such unsubstantiated thoughts can soon become familiar and eventually unquestioned. Some traditions are incidental, and make little difference. But when dealing with biblical accuracy, it is a good idea to assume it is relevant.

I have always loved the story of the visit of the magi. That visit is the subject of this book. That visit is full of intrigue, diabolical plots, divine rescue, mysterious people, and personality studies. In it, we see the overarching providence of God. However, there are few stories that are overlaid with more tradition than this story. I think some clarification as to what is biblical and what is traditional is in order. I am not doing this to throw cold water on familiar Christmas traditions. I am not trying to bring critique to commonly sung carols or to nativity scenes showing possibly inaccurate circumstances. I still sing those songs, and we still display multiple nativities around our house at Christmas. But I have found a new magic in Christmas based on biblical accuracy that I believe brings a greater intrigue than some of the traditions give. God has chosen to invade our world of time and location and to work in historical context to reveal himself. Our highest joy in contemplating biblical stories should come from an accurate understanding of scriptural truth. So, this is written not simply to create a critical perspective, but to increase our joy in discerning biblical fact from fiction.

Of the four gospel accounts, only Luke and Matthew give any historical detail about the nativity. Luke alone tells of the angels appearing to the shepherds. Matthew's gospel is the only place in the Bible that tells of the visit of the magi. The narratives quoted in this book will thus mostly come from Matthew, Chapter 2.

Fact or Assumption?
In the following chapters I intend to propose a few things that may be new ideas for you. I will give supporting evidence of them. My proposed conclusions may not be explicitly stated in scripture. Therefore, I cannot call them "fact." However, I will attempt to show that they are implicitly supported, and are more likely than the traditional views. Don't worry. We won't be knocking out any pillars of the faith. We will be dealing with details, but I think these details will enhance our view of the God of providence. We will try to view this story in light of the big picture of redemption, and I believe accuracy in our understanding of the details will serve that end.

Why am I writing this? To get closer to what I believe is the narrative truth given in scripture. The last chapter of this book will summarize some implications of these interpretations. First, we must make our suggested distinctions between biblically stated or implied facts and traditional assumptions.

Style of This Book

I don't bring much extraneous jargon into this little book. My observations are focused and stated as succinctly as I know how. The chapters are very short and to-the-point. They are topically structured for rational thought progression. This is not a report of research into extra-biblical material. My observations are coming straight from scriptural investigation, except that brief reference is occasionally made to general historical knowledge giving support for the validity of my logic.

I hope this book arouses a renewed enjoyment of this favorite Christmas story. Further, I hope it serves to remind ourselves that scripture is our best commentary on scripture if we invest ourselves to knowing it.

Chapter 2

Who Were these Wise Men?

Matthew 2:1-3 (NKJV)
[1] Now after Jesus was born in Bethlehem of Judea in the days of Herod the king, behold, wise men from the East came to Jerusalem, [2] saying, "Where is He who has been born King of the Jews? For we have seen His star in the East and have come to worship Him." [3] When Herod the king heard this, he was troubled, and all Jerusalem with him.

The wise men, also sometimes translated *magi*, have always had an aura of mystery about them. They came from *the East*, from an unnamed country. They appeared suddenly, drew much royal attention, then disappeared from our observation forever. The Christmas carol calls them "we three kings."

The East means, of course, east from Jerusalem, and from Judea. That takes us most probably across the Arabian desert to the land of Mesopotamia. This is a strip of land roughly surrounding the Tigris and Euphrates rivers in present-day Iraq. A lot of fanciful speculation exists about who the magi were. Our first objective is to try to identify them from a more biblical logic.

To do this, we first need to sweep through a little ancient biblical history. Following the great flood in the days of Noah, people began to multiply and migrate southeastward from the mountains of Ararat in today's Turkey, following the Tigris-Euphrates river valley. The earliest post-flood civilizations began there. Something else began there. The overt practice of idolatry seems to have originated in this setting. Moving quickly through time, we encounter the rise of the Assyrian and Chaldean empires. These two idolatrous nations were neighbors, and became territorial rivals, the Assyrians located generally northward from the Chaldeans. Dominion switched back and forth between them over several centuries. In the latter part of the 7th century B.C. with the Babylonians in dominant power in the land of the Chaldees', the Babylonian king Nebuchadnezzar began a campaign of conquest. He reached Israel about 607 B.C. The chosen people were conquered and the 'choice' people of Judah were exiled to Babylon to serve the king. Among those captured was Daniel, and the entire book of prophecy bearing his name was written during exile. Daniel's excellent divine wisdom soon gained him great favor with the king.

In Daniel, chapter two opens with Nebuchadnezzar's famous dream. Here is the account:

Daniel 2:1-3 (ESV)
¹ In the second year of the reign of Nebuchadnezzar, Nebuchadnezzar had dreams; his spirit was troubled, and his sleep left him. ² Then the king commanded that the magicians, the enchanters, the sorcerers, and the Chaldeans be summoned to tell the king his dreams. So they came in and stood before the king. ³ And the king said to them, "I had a dream, and my spirit is troubled to know the dream."

If you do not know the rest of the story, you should read it in its entirety, but the important thing for us to note here is the identity of the men the king called in to consult. Biblical and extra-biblical evidence shows that there existed within Babylon a caste of men who were considered wise. They were very well educated and spent their lives in pursuit of knowledge. They gained it from many sources. They eagerly learned from people they conquered, integrating their wisdom into their own. They maintained a library of documents, including those from captured peoples. From this position of attributed wisdom, they served as royal advisors. Thus, they no doubt had studied from Hebrew literature, including their prophetic proclamations. It was common knowledge in the region at that time that Israel had a legacy of prophets that could ascertain secrets, interpret dreams, and predict the future.

Besides their thirst for learning from written literature, they also, being idolatrous as they were, involved themselves in astrology. The latter of the four consultant groups mentioned in the scripture above is *Chaldeans*. Some translations render this Greek word 'astrologers,' for the Chaldeans were particularly characterized by their superstitious stargazing. Other groups of the king's advisors are the *magicians* who seemed to defy natural experience, and the *enchanters* and *sorcerers* who claimed to contact the underworld and the afterlife. Together they embodied an impressive collection of 'wisdom' of all sorts. These wise men were elite in their culture, and were employed in the selection and approving of the kings of Babylon. Thus, they enjoyed the esteem and political power of nobility. Because of his demonstrated prophetic wisdom and the power of his God through him, Daniel was made leader over this powerful group by Nebuchadnezzar and was second only to the king himself.

This caste of wise men seems to have survived several changes of political dynasties. After the Babylonians were conquered by the Meads and Persians in about 538 B.C., Daniel and the caste of wise men remained as royal advisors to the Persian conquerors, as seen in Daniel 6. With Daniel as their leader, it is probable that they learned something of Jewish scripture. The prophetic legacy brought credence, and Daniel's well-known spirit of prophecy gave evidence to this source of wisdom. Thus, the forerunners of the magi would have learned it first-hand from a real Jewish prophet.

In the time of Jesus' birth more than 500 years later, these *magi* were still there, still functioning as royal hierarchy, and apparently wielding great influence in their culture. The term *magi* derives from the same root word as 'magician.' It was used by the gospel-writer Matthew to include generally the whole caste of the wise men: the magicians, the enchanters, the sorcerers, and the astrologers. They saw a star, which to them, signaled the birth of a new king. Thus, although not specifically stated in the Bible, it seems highly likely that the magi were from the land and cultures of the Medes and Persians, the Babylonians before them, and the Chaldeans still earlier. Later, during the times of the apostolic church, it is possible that the influence of this culture was still existent in the account in Acts of Paul and Barnabas' journey to Cyprus.

> *Acts 13:5-6 (ESV)*
> [5] *When they arrived at Salamis, they proclaimed the word of God in the synagogues of the Jews. And they had John to assist them.* [6] *When they had gone through the whole island as far as Paphos, they came upon a certain magician, a Jewish false prophet named Bar-Jesus.*

(Salamis is a city in Cyprus. John is John Mark, later author of the Gospel of Mark.) The magic arts performed by Bar-Jesus possibly had their roots in past wise men of Mesopotamia.

If this is an accurate identity of the magi, it seems remarkable that they would travel from Persia to Palestine to pay homage to a Jewish king. It is true that this is what they did occasionally, but to travel to such a distant soil, and into such a different religious culture still seems over the top. Yet, that is precisely what is reported in Matthew's gospel. It is likely that from what they understood by studying Jewish prophecy from the perspective of an outsider, they made that trip.

Non-biblical traditions have assigned names and diverse origins to the magi. These are completely unsubstantiated by scripture—another example of tradition that must be stripped away to better seek scriptural truth. It seems more logical that they all came from a common location such that they could easily collaborate in research. None of these men could have individually done the thorough investigation necessary to make this journey in just a few months. It had to be a large group effort.

The fact that these magi made this unlikely journey, and that it is recorded in New Testament scripture, introduces the idea that perhaps they were being summoned by God Himself. This will be further established later in this book, but for now, let us begin to view this journey of the magi as a divine call. The first question that arises is,

"Why?" One thing is certain. God crossed ethnic, cultural, and religious boundaries in their calling. He overlooked their idolatrous background, their superstitious astrology, and even utilized these backgrounds to woo them. If God was calling them, he reached out to that far corridor to gather worshippers from those far away. The magi expended great time, effort, cost, and personal security to pursue such a journey of faith toward a God who was not their own.

How many magi were there? Since three gifts are mentioned in the Matthew narrative, tradition has assumed there were three magi. Songs speak of "We three kings", and traditional nativity scenes without fail have three magi figures. Scripturally there could have been three or ten or more. Three is as good an assumption as any, but the biblical narrative does not tell how many there were. However, it is highly unlikely that three high-ranking eastern nobles would make such a long and dangerous journey alone. Whatever their numbers were, they likely had a formidable attachment of Persian soldiers guarding them and many attending servants. Thus, when they entered Jerusalem, it was no doubt with much fanfare.

Understanding all this effort and risk required to make this journey, we are prodded to wonder if we are as hungry for the truth as they were? Are we exhausting all reliable means to better connect with the Divine? Do we study our Bible to know God with the intensity of these wise men? This story is very compelling, when comparing the seeking hearts of the magi with the indifference of the populace of Jerusalem. When the Jerusalem inhabitants heard the message of a possible messianic birth, they apparently didn't bother to trek four miles to Bethlehem to check it out. We each must ask ourselves, "Which one am I; the seeking pilgrim or the complacent resident?"

Chapter 3
The Journey of the Magi

The Route
We often picture the magi crossing desert sand dunes on their camels with the star shining brightly in the distance, guiding them on. If they traveled straight across the Arabian Desert, the journey would span about 500-600 miles, depending on the location of its origin. However, that would have not been the normal route of travel. It is more likely that they traveled northwestward along the Tigris-Euphrates river valley, then turned southwestward toward the land of Palestine. This would follow the 'fertile crescent' of the region, a well-populated trade route. It would have been safer, and would have had intermediate provisions for food and water. This route would have covered about 1000 miles.

Matthew 2:3-9 (NKJV)
³ When Herod the king heard this, he was troubled, and all Jerusalem with him. ⁴ And when he had gathered all the chief priests and scribes of the people together, he inquired of them where the Christ was to be born. ⁵ So they said to him, "In Bethlehem of Judea, for thus it is written by the prophet: ⁶ 'But you, Bethlehem, in the land of Judah, Are not the least among the rulers of Judah; For out of you shall come a Ruler Who will shepherd My people Israel.' " ⁷ Then Herod, when he had secretly called the wise men, determined from them what time the star appeared. ⁸ And he sent them to Bethlehem and said, "Go and search carefully for the young Child, and when you have found Him, bring back word to me, that I may come and worship Him also." ⁹ When they heard the king, they departed; . . .

The two legs of the magi's journey that are noted in scripture are from *the East* to Jerusalem, a distance of about a thousand miles, and then from Jerusalem to Nazareth, a trip of seventy-five to a hundred miles depending on their route. (Luke 2:39 tells us that by the time of the magi's visit, the little family had returned to their home in Nazareth. Their return would have begun a minimum of forty-one days after childbirth in order to dedicate Jesus as a firstborn son and to complete Mary's purification rites, allowing her to travel home from Bethlehem and Jerusalem. During that forty-plus days, the little family dwelt in Bethlehem. Luke 2:24 further tells us that Joseph and Mary brought a purification offering of two domestic birds. According to Mosaic requirement given in Leviticus 12, a sacrificial lamb was to be offered, but if the woman could not afford a lamb, she could bring either two doves or two young pigeons. On this basis we conclude that Joseph and Mary were relatively poor--not the bottom of their society since Joseph had a profession, but they were nonetheless peasants. It was on this occasion that the holy family encountered Simeon and Anna at the temple as reported in Luke 2:22-40.)

As we develop the events, it will be helpful to understand these relative distances. We would expect the magi's trip from *the East* to Jerusalem to require months of travel. In contrast, the trip from Jerusalem to Nazareth would require only a few days. Jerusalem was a bustling city with high walls and gates. Nazareth, on the other hand, was a small village. Nothing is said in the biblical narrative, but we can imagine that this caravan that turned heads in Jerusalem now created quite an air of wonder for these remote villagers when this imposing entourage came to visit their quiet little town.

Mode of Travel
The scripture does not tell us how these magi and their cohorts traveled. Was it by camel as often is assumed? Or was it by horseback or even by foot? Camels were better suited to long dry trips, but if they followed the trade routes, that may not have been an issue. Camels remain a probable assumption, perhaps with servants on foot.

Delay before Travel
The elapsed time between the magi first seeing the star and beginning their journey is unknown. We can only speculate on the likely. Even

if their superstitious interpretive methods caused them to immediately connect the star sighting to an upcoming king, still we can imagine they had some collaboration to do. Then we should expect some research time while they checked their library archives. Once they connected it with the nation of Israel, they would require more research and some time for trip preparation. Thus, it is reasonable to expect some time to have elapsed after first seeing the star before they started on their journey. Notice that when Herod questioned the magi secretly, he didn't ask how long they had been traveling, but how long since they first saw the star. Those two times could have differed significantly.

It is rather amazing that God spoke to them within their own pagan culture, using even their own idolatrous beliefs to convince them of the truth of the birth of the King of kings. This is not unique in history. Missionaries to other cultures frequently discover symbolisms of biblical truth, even gospel truth, embedded in those cultures. God reaches out with His message where he wishes. and he prepares an avenue of entrance so that a foothold can be gained by those who are sent. God is a seeking God.

Chapter 4

Prophecy in Their Heads

As mentioned in the previous chapter, it is probable that after the magi saw the star, they did some research. Evidence exits showing that the Chaldeans believed that the prognosis of the rise of kings and dynasties was written in the stars. In their thirst for knowledge, they searched not only their own traditions, but also those of the peoples they conquered. They probably searched through the Hebrew scriptures looking for information about a future king. Not just any king, but a significant king. If that is so, then their thirst was sumptuously whetted by all the messianic prophecies in the Jewish scriptures—which for us is the Old Testament.

<u>Messianic Prophecies</u>
For these wise men, Hebrew prophecy was a cache of wisdom just begging for understanding. This prophecy had a legacy of being historically relevant and much of it had since been fulfilled, adding to its credence as a treasure of wisdom and revealer of mysteries. Their own ancestors had first-hand experience with Daniel and his prophetic wisdom. They had seen his accurate interpretation of other prophecies. Likely, this legacy of knowledge was passed down, and they eagerly devoured the Hebrew scriptures looking for specific connections to a future king.

As the wise men searched, they likely found many references about a future person of significance—the promised Messiah. They probably were perplexed by the dichotomy of roles prophesied for Messiah. After all, even the Jewish leaders down through history, and including those of Jesus' day, had not solved this dichotomy. The majority of their scriptures pointed to Messiah as a victorious king and leader of the people, but some portrayed him as a suffering servant, one acquainted with sorrow, and some as a priest. We have no record of which scriptures they identified, but it is logical to assume they saw some of the more obvious ones. Assuming thorough investigation with the help of many investigators, here are a few they might have found describing his victorious kingship.

Psalm 2:6-12 (ESV)
[6] "As for me, I have set my King on Zion, my holy hill." [7] I will tell of the decree: The LORD said to me, "You are my Son; today I have begotten you. [8] Ask of me, and I will make the nations your heritage, and the ends of the earth your possession. [9] You shall break them with a rod of iron and dash them in pieces like a potter's vessel." [10] Now therefore, O kings, be wise; be warned, O rulers of the earth. [11] Serve the LORD with fear, and rejoice with trembling. [12] Kiss the Son, lest he be angry, and you perish in the way, for his wrath is quickly kindled. Blessed are all who take refuge in him.

Daniel 2:44 (ESV)
[44] And in the days of those kings the God of heaven will set up a kingdom that shall never be destroyed, nor shall the kingdom be left to another people. It shall break in pieces all these kingdoms and bring them to an end, and it shall stand forever,

Isaiah 9:6-7 (ESV)
[6] For to us a child is born, to us a son is given; and the government shall be upon his shoulder, and his name shall be called Wonderful Counselor, Mighty God, Everlasting Father, Prince of Peace. [7] Of the increase of his government and of peace there will be no end, on the throne of David and over his kingdom, to establish it and to uphold it with justice and with righteousness from this time forth and forevermore. The zeal of the LORD of hosts will do this.

Daniel 7:13-14 (ESV)
[13] "I saw in the night visions, and behold, with the clouds of heaven there came one like a son of man, and he came to the

Ancient of Days and was presented before him. [14] *And to him was given dominion and glory and a kingdom, that all peoples, nations, and languages should serve him; his dominion is an everlasting dominion, which shall not pass away, and his kingdom one that shall not be destroyed.*

Jeremiah 23:5-6 (ESV)
[5] *"Behold, the days are coming, declares the LORD, when I will raise up for David a righteous Branch, and he shall reign as king and deal wisely, and shall execute justice and righteousness in the land.* [6] *In his days Judah will be saved, and Israel will dwell securely. And this is the name by which he will be called: 'The LORD is our righteousness.'*

Note the recurring theme stating that this kingdom is an everlasting kingdom, one for which there is no end. In contrast, all other kingdoms will be destroyed. This aspect would undoubtedly have been of immense interest to this caste of 'kingmakers.' Additionally, they may have read some passages linking his royal role with a priestly role.

Psalm 110:4 (ESV)
[4] *The LORD has sworn and will not change his mind, "You are a priest forever after the order of Melchizedek."*

Zechariah 6:12-13 (ESV)
[12] *And say to him, 'Thus says the LORD of hosts, "Behold, the man whose name is the Branch: for he shall branch out from his place, and he shall build the temple of the LORD.* [13] *It is he who shall build the temple of the LORD and shall bear royal honor, and shall sit and rule on his throne. And there shall be a priest on his throne, and the counsel of peace shall be between them both."'*

The wise men probably also read some passages that spoke of his more humble role as 'prince of peace,' even as a suffering one.

Zechariah 9:9 (ESV)
⁹ Rejoice greatly, O daughter of Zion! Shout aloud, O daughter of Jerusalem! Behold, your king is coming to you; righteous and having salvation is he, humble and mounted on a donkey, on a colt, the foal of a donkey.

Isaiah 53:1-12 (ESV)
¹ Who has believed what he has heard from us? And to whom has the arm of the LORD been revealed? ² For he grew up before him like a young plant, and like a root out of dry ground; he had no form or majesty that we should look at him, and no beauty that we should desire him. ³ He was despised and rejected by men; a man of sorrows, and acquainted with grief; and as one from whom men hide their faces he was despised, and we esteemed him not. ⁴ Surely he has borne our griefs and carried our sorrows; yet we esteemed him stricken, smitten by God, and afflicted. ⁵ But he was pierced for our transgressions; he was crushed for our iniquities; upon him was the chastisement that brought us peace, and with his wounds we are healed. ⁶ All we like sheep have gone astray; we have turned—every one—to his own way; and the LORD has laid on him the iniquity of us all. ⁷ He was oppressed, and he was afflicted, yet he opened not his mouth; like a lamb that is led to the slaughter, and like a sheep that before its shearers is silent, so he opened not his mouth. ⁸ By oppression and judgment he was taken away; and as for his generation, who considered that he was cut off out of the land of the living, stricken for the transgression of my people? ⁹ And they made his grave with the wicked and with a rich man in his death, although he had done no violence, and there was no deceit in his mouth. ¹⁰ Yet it was the will of the LORD to crush him; he has put him to grief; when his soul makes an offering for guilt, he shall see his offspring; he shall prolong his days; the will of the LORD shall prosper in his hand. ¹¹ Out of the anguish of his soul he shall see and be satisfied; by his knowledge shall the

righteous one, my servant, make many to be accounted righteous, and he shall bear their iniquities. [12] *Therefore I will divide him a portion with the many, and he shall divide the spoil with the strong, because he poured out his soul to death and was numbered with the transgressors; yet he bore the sin of many, and makes intercession for the transgressors.*

One Key Prophecy?

One other prophecy may have been instrumental in motivating the magi's visit. It was proclaimed earlier in Israel's history than most of the other prophecies. It is most interesting to the story of the magi because it was a prophecy given by a Gentile prophet. As the magi read this, they were receiving a Gentile-to-Gentile prophecy coming right out of the Jewish scriptures! Near the end of the exodus wanderings, the nation of Israel had finally crossed from the Sinai Desert into the land across the Jordan. They approached Moab to pass through the land. However, the Moabites were terrified, for they had just seen Israel defeat the mighty Amorites. The king of Moab sent for Balaam, a known 'prophet,' to pronounce a curse over the nation of Israel, offering to pay him a handsome reward. So Balaam inquired of the Lord Almighty and the Lord gave him five prophetic oracles. The oracles were a blessing over Israel rather than a curse. Buried in these oracles, Balaam was given a wonderful glimpse of the messianic purpose (which was to be the ultimate goal of this whole matter.)

Numbers 24:17 (ESV)
[17] *I see him, but not now; I behold him, but not near: a star shall come out of Jacob, and a scepter shall rise out of Israel; . . .*

One might be inclined to ignore this prophecy. After all, the prophet Balaam is not spoken of favorably by New Testament writers.

2 Peter 2:15 (ESV)
[15] *Forsaking the right way, they have gone astray. They have followed the way of Balaam, the son of Beor, who loved gain from wrongdoing,*

Jude 1:11 (ESV)
¹¹ Woe to them! For they walked in the way of Cain and abandoned themselves for the sake of gain to Balaam's error and perished in Korah's rebellion.

Revelation 2:14 (ESV)
¹⁴ But I have a few things against you: you have some there who hold the teaching of Balaam, who taught Balak to put a stumbling block before the sons of Israel, so that they might eat food sacrificed to idols and practice sexual immorality.

That is what makes this prophecy so intriguing. At the coming of Jesus, God was willing to use an unfavorable Gentile prophet, and to reach to a pagan culture to proclaim the good news. What a divine message of grace!

Since the Israelites were not stargazers, they would have understood the star of this prophecy as purely symbolic for a new king. These magi, on the other hand, would likely have interpreted that a literal *star* would shine forth the signal of a new king. Combining their astrological bent with their strong respect for the Hebrew prophecies, they may have been convinced this was that moment in time predicted by the many passages they had discovered. The appearance of the star had incited their quest. We don't know how informed they were about the prophecies before seeing the star, but it is highly likely they researched intently the Hebrew scriptures and become educated in knowledge they lacked. What they discovered motivated them to make their tremendous journey.

Behind-the-Scene
I hope that by now we are seeing the journey of the magi as not merely an interesting turn of events, but as an orchestration of history by God to bring it about. His providence in the affairs of men is unmistakable. God is a calling God. What was God's purpose in this journey? It may have opened hearts in Persia for later receiving the Gospel. One message is being clearly made to us through this journey. God was

reaching across cultural and religious barriers. Jesus, the Messiah of Israel, had a broader purpose for the Gospel than just for saving Israel. It is revealed often in the Old Testament, but nowhere more clearly than in this intimate dialog within the Trinity prior to the first advent of Jesus, and revealed to Isaiah the prophet.

Isaiah 49:5-6 (ESV)
[5] And now the LORD says, he who formed me from the womb to be his servant, to bring Jacob back to him; and that Israel might be gathered to him— for I am honored in the eyes of the LORD, and my God has become my strength— [6] he says: "It is too light a thing that you should be my servant to raise up the tribes of Jacob and to bring back the preserved of Israel; I will make you as a light for the nations, that my salvation may reach to the end of the earth."

What a message for this largely Gentile world! The magi must have tingled when they read of the outreaching nature of the Hebrew God. God broke down barriers and he calls us to do the same. Often the greatest barriers we must break down are those of our own building, barriers of prejudice, fear, or comfort. We must journey from our comfort zone to the risky realm of being vulnerable before the world, just as the magi did. Are we seeking the King with the same resolve as those magi?

Chapter 5

The Magi Encounter Jerusalem

Why did the magi go first to Jerusalem? The only logical answer is their assumption that this royal child had been born to the royal family in the capital city. They fully expected King Herod to receive their goodwill visit with appreciation. They did not expect their announcement of purpose to surprise the king. The very entrance of this troupe of Persian nobles, together with their military and supportive entourage, must itself have turned a few heads. Matthew instructs his reader to *behold* this majestic entrance. Behold indeed! This arrival was a jaw-dropping occasion in just its appearance. No doubt, the Persian military presence must have raised the angst of the occupying Romans. There could even have been enough of them to outnumber the Roman occupational forces--this is unknown. It stirred the entire city hastily. There was another reason why.

Matthew 2:1-8 (NKJV)
[1] Now after Jesus was born in Bethlehem of Judea in the days of Herod the king, behold, wise men from the East came to Jerusalem, [2] saying, "Where is He who has been born King of the Jews? For we have seen His star in the East and have come to worship Him." [3] When Herod the king heard this, he was troubled, and all Jerusalem with him. [4] And when he had gathered all the chief priests and scribes of the people together, he inquired of them where the Christ was to be born. [5] So they said to him, "In Bethlehem of Judea, for thus it is written by the prophet: [6] 'But you, Bethlehem, in the land of Judah, Are not the least among the rulers of Judah; For out of you shall come a Ruler Who will shepherd My people Israel.' " [7] Then Herod, when he had secretly called the wise men, determined from them what time the star appeared. [8] And he sent them to Bethlehem and said, "Go and search carefully for the young Child, and

when you have found Him, bring back word to me, that I may come and worship Him also."

This passage shows that neither Herod nor the magi knew the specific birthplace of Jesus. Herod inquired of the chief priests and the scribes where the promised Messiah was to be born. They quoted to him from Micah 5:2. The small village of Bethlehem was well known as the birthplace of King David in the Old Testament. It lay just about four miles south of Jerusalem. Micah prophesied many years after David lived and was therefore referring to a future king. Jesus was a descendent of David on both his mother's side and on Joseph's side, as attested by the genealogies given in Matthew 1 and Luke 3. This Davidic descendancy was a necessary prerequisite of the prophesied Messiah. During his ministry, he was frequently called *Son of David* by the common people.

Why was Herod *troubled and all Jerusalem with him*? 'Herod the Great,' as he has been called, was the first in a line of kings in Israel under the name Herod. He was Idumean in ethnicity, meaning he was half Jewish and half Moabite. In his ambition to seize power in Palestine, he convinced Augustus Caesar in Rome that he was well-qualified by his Jewish connection to lead Israel and to make them loyal to Rome. He was never well-received by the Jewish community. The Jewish leaders accommodated him out of necessity, but they considered him an illegitimate king since he was not a full-blood son of David, as foretold to David by the Lord through the prophet Nathan:

2 Samuel 7:16-17 (NKJV)
[16] And your house and your kingdom shall be established forever before you. Your throne shall be established forever."
[17] According to all these words and according to all this vision, so Nathan spoke to David.

Herod had ruled in Palestine for over 40 years, during which he was an aggressive builder, constructing Roman-style cities throughout Israel. The quality of his building was unmatched in that day. Archaeologists can often recognize and distinguish Herodian structures by their perfection. To appease the Jews for his Roman loyalties, Herod refurbished their mighty temple, the one standing during Jesus' earthly lifetime and during the early apostolic church.

Herod had a maniacal ambition and a severe paranoia about losing his power. He had ten wives, all of whom bore him sons, and all of whom aspired their son to inherit the throne. We know from extra-biblical sources that he executed his most beloved wife Mariamne, his mother-in-law, his brother-in-law, and three of his sons for subversive plots or rumors of such plots.

Herod was well aware of the prejudice of the orthodox Jews against him, which incited his paranoia even more. When he heard from the magi of a possible competitor for the throne of Israel, he immediately felt threatened. It was consistent with his character to plot the death of this competitor. What Herod was feeling seems vastly understated by the word *troubled*. He was immediately afraid and furious.

Why was all Jerusalem *troubled* along with Herod? Because of his history. He had a reputation of dealing ruthlessly with the Jews and had slaughtered many in retaliation against opposition. The people held Herod to be a mad man, and they knew that when Herod wasn't happy, heads would roll.

> *Matthew 2:13-18 (NKJV)*
> *[13] Now when they had departed, behold, an angel of the Lord appeared to Joseph in a dream, saying, "Arise, take the young Child and His mother, flee to Egypt, and stay there until I bring you word; for Herod will seek the young Child to destroy Him."*
> *[14] When he arose, he took the young Child and His mother by night and departed for Egypt, [15] and was there until the death of Herod, that it might be fulfilled which was spoken by the Lord through the prophet, saying, "Out of Egypt I called My Son."*
> *[16] Then Herod, when he saw that he was deceived by the wise men, was exceedingly angry; and he sent forth and put to death*

all the male children who were in Bethlehem and in all its districts, from two years old and under, according to the time which he had determined from the wise men. ^{17} Then was fulfilled what was spoken by Jeremiah the prophet, saying: ^{18} "A voice was heard in Ramah, Lamentation, weeping, and great mourning, Rachel weeping for her children, refusing to be comforted, because they are no more."

The Timing

Although all of Jerusalem sensed Herod's troubled spirit, apparently he concealed it well from the visiting magi. He feigned a sincere desire to worship the child. He used this pretense to meet secretly with them to get information. It is clear from his question to them that his plot was already formulated. He wanted to know when the star first appeared so that he could judge the age of the child he was looking for. Their answer is not given, but we have a semblance of a time frame in the fact that he later gave orders to kill all boys two years of age and younger. (My guess is that Jesus was roughly one year old at the time of the magi's visit and that Herod added some contingency to make sure he killed this new royal challenger. One year would have given sufficient time for the magi to have done their research, prepared for their travel, and made the journey.

Despite this plotting and unrest in the mind of Herod, the magi apparently never suspected ill-will. Herod was a skilled schemer. They probably anticipated a more principled and graceful king in Israel. Herod concealed any appearance to the contrary. The magi had to later be warned by God through a dream not to return to Herod.

Chapter 6
The Star

One of the wonders of this story is the mysterious star. Our Christmas cards and children's picture books depict this ultra-bright star with a peculiar beam shining down upon a tiny stable. What this star was, and how it might have come about, has been the speculation of well-intentioned historians and pseudo-scientists. We are caused to believe through our Christmas traditions that the magi set out from Persia using this star as their guide. The star is typically envisioned as a stellar signal to the whole surrounding world that something special was going on in Bethlehem. We often find ourselves swept along with these traditions without taking time to compare with what we are reading in scripture. Yet, we might easily question when we sing (from the First Noel):

"They looked up and saw a star,
shining in the east beyond them far."

And then follow that by singing (from We Three Kings):

"Westward leading, still proceeding
Guide us to thy perfect light."

-- if the star is in the east, why are they traveling west? We will attempt to set straight some of these traditions, problems, and speculations in this chapter; to fearlessly challenge some very entrenched assumptions.

The Brilliance of the Star
Our first challenge is that almost without exception, any visual portrayal of the star of Bethlehem shows it to be shining with exceptional brightness, easily surpassing all surrounding stars. It is seen as a beacon of hope to a dark and lost world. Anyone in the area would have to take note of its brilliance and wonder at its glory.

Christmas cards often show shepherds in a field with Bethlehem in the distance, with the giant star overhead, casting its spotlight on the town. Is all that scriptural?

One question needs to be asked. Based on the scriptural record, besides the magi, who else saw the star? The answer is that no one else is reported seeing the star. Not the shepherds. Not the Jerusalem guards or town's people. Not the religious leaders. Not the inn-keeper. Not Mary and Joseph. No one. Why? Because the Jewish people were not stargazers. If it had been an unmistakable phenomenon, everyone would have seen it. As it is, no one else is reported to have seen it. It probably was not a sign to the surrounding world. It seems as if it were only a sign to the magi and not to anyone else in that day.

Besides the reference to a star in Balaam's prophecy that we discussed in chapter 4, a couple of clearly messianic references in scripture are made to a morning star.

2 Peter 1:19 (ESV)
And we have the prophetic word more fully confirmed, to which you will do well to pay attention as to a lamp shining in a dark place, until the day dawns and the morning star rises in your hearts,

Revelation 2:26-28 (NIV)
[26] To the one who is victorious and does my will to the end, I will give authority over the nations— [27] that one 'will rule them with an iron scepter and will dash them to pieces like pottery'—just as I have received authority from my Father. [28] I will also give that one the morning star.

A morning star seems to symbolize significant glory. The term was even applied to Lucifer before his fall.

Isaiah 14:12 (NIV)
[12] How you have fallen from heaven, morning star, son of the dawn! You have been cast down to the earth, you who once laid low the nations!

In the closing verses of the book of Revelation (and of the Bible itself), John heard Jesus claim:

Revelation 22:16b (NKJV)
[16] "...I am the Root and the Offspring of David, the Bright and Morning Star."

In our understanding, a morning star is one that is bright enough that it continues to shine past the first dawning of daybreak. We often see one today. It may be unusually bright, but it is not uniquely noteworthy. We usually identify a morning star as one of the planets when we see one. While they are interesting, they are not uncommon. If it is true that only the magi took note of the star, then I suggest that the star, while maybe notably brighter than average, was not phenomenal in brightness. The magi saw it because they were constantly scanning and studying the stars. They readily identified a star that had not existed the night before or any other night. An experienced stargazer might take note, but it would not be a cause for excitement to the average Jewish observer. As we have said, no one else is reported in Scripture as having noticed it.

Based on the long-standing assumption that the star was an exceptional phenomenon, much speculation has tried to explain the star in terms of a natural happenstance. Attempts have been made to identify it as Halley's comet, or some other comet, or as an alignment of several bright stars. However, attempts at back-tracing of the time frame does not match any known such events.

More convincingly, simple logic might observe that if it was purely a natural phenomenon, then the star would move from east to west with the other stars as the earth's rotation takes it through its stellar trajectory. What might start out in the east, would eventually end up in the west, then disappear, only to reappear the next night in the east again. If the wise men were following the star, it would be hard to follow without traveling in circles. This thinking seems to make the magi following a star of natural phenomenon rather absurd. This leaves two options. Either the star was not a natural phenomenon, or the magi were not following the star. I suggest that both are true.

A Proposed Star Scenario

Allow me to propose a star-sighting scenario that I believe is consistent with this scripture passage. Then I will suggest some supporting evidences from the passage itself.

First, remember that there were two legs to this journey. It will be helpful to keep in mind the relative distances. From Persia to Jerusalem it was roughly 1,000 miles, and from Jerusalem to Nazareth, about seventy-five miles. I believe the star appeared to the magi in the sky on the night that Jesus was born, then soon disappeared from view. We don't know at that first sighting how long it shown, if it was stationary, or if it moved with the other stars across the night sky. Based on the star's later behavior, it could very well have moved independently, differentiating itself in that way from the other stars. If it was independent, we assume it was likely positioned in the direction of Israel. One thing we do know. It appeared where no star had existed the night before, and I propose that it disappeared as suddenly, only shining for a short time, maybe just that one night. The magi did not see the star again during the months of contemplating, planning and preparing, nor during their journey from Persia to Jerusalem. When they left Jerusalem, sent by Herod southward to Bethlehem, the star reappeared and redirected their journey northward to Nazareth. It moved ahead of them and came to rest in a manner that led them to the very house where Jesus was, with his parents. At least during this short period of time, we are clearly told that this star did not move with the other stars, but was independent of them. Here are reasons why I propose this scenario.

The Geography

If you are like me, maps are a great help. In this case, the relative geography is so simple you can just imagine it. Jerusalem and the land of Palestine are in the western part, on the left side of your imaginary map. Persia is on the eastern portion, or the right side, of the map. Now the problem. The scripture says, *For we have seen His star in the East and have come to worship Him.* If they were in Persia, on the right side of your map, and the star is east from there, that puts it farther to the right, opposite the direction of Jerusalem and Bethlehem.

The Greek word for *east* in the early scripture manuscripts is *anatolē* in English spelling. It is literally translated *uprising,* implying [*of the sun*]. Its usage in the New Testament (and for its Old Testament counterpart as well) consistently shows that its normal sense simply means 'the eastern direction'. In this Matthew passage, this same word is used twice. The first usage tells us that *wise men came from the East.* The second usage says they *had seen his star in the East.* The same Greek word for east is used in both uses.

This east star has posed such a dilemma that many modern translations have adopted the literal translation of the word for its second usage in this verse, rather than the normal meaning of it. They translate it literally as *we have seen his star at its rising,* or *as it arose,* or something similar. The English Standard Version uses this convention. Older issues of the New International Version rendered it *in the east,* but the 2011 issue has switched to *at its rising.* That is why I chose the New King James Version for this specific text rendering. It is consistent with the normal usage in the original language. I don't think this newer translation stems from improved linguistics, but from the dilemma with the directions. Otherwise, why didn't they translate it the same way both times it was used in the same verse? This does not indicate an error in translation, but it does show a tension in its understanding.

I have adopted this less prevalent solution to the problem. I suggest that when the magi made this statement, they were telling us both when and where they were when they saw the star. I believe it should be understood as, *For we have seen His star* [while we were] *in the East and have come to worship Him.* I believe *in the East* refers to the location of the magi when the star appeared to them, not the location of the star. If this is so, it also tells us when they saw the star. They saw it while they were *in the East*, that is, before their journey began. This proposal is not unsupported. The following additional arguments support this understanding.

Tense
Notice that their seeing of the star is in past tense regarding its sighting. *We have seen . . .* They did not say, *we see his star,* or *we are seeing his star.* They had seen it. Past tense. Their sighting of the star was clearly stated as in the past.

Missing Testimony
No mention is made of the magi calling Herod out into the courtyard and pointing out the star. This would have seemed like an important thing to do to establish their legitimacy. They couldn't point to it if the seeing of the star was already in the past.

Misdirection by the Star?
Since the star somehow eventually led the Magi to the precise house where Jesus was, why did they go to Jerusalem and ask his whereabouts? If they were following the star all along, this would make no sense. Assuming they were following the trade route, they would have passed near Nazareth before arriving at Jerusalem. And why ask where the child was if they knew the star was leading them elsewhere? If they were following a precision-guided path between Persia and Jerusalem, that would seem illogical. However, we have already stated that their asking probably came from a preexisting assumption that he was to be found in the capital city of Jerusalem. That assumption only makes sense if they were not currently following the star. Thus, the fact that they bypassed Nazareth and journeyed on

to Jerusalem and inquired about Messiah is support for the proposal that they were not following the star from Persia to Jerusalem.

The Joy of the Magi

Matthew 2:8-10 (NKJV)
[8] And he sent them to Bethlehem and said, "Go and search carefully for the young Child, and when you have found Him, bring back word to me, that I may come and worship Him also." [9] When they heard the king, they departed; and behold, the star which they had seen in the East went before them, till it came and stood over where the young Child was. [10] When they saw the star, they rejoiced with exceedingly great joy.

Why did the magi rejoice *with exceedingly great joy*? If they had been seeing the star and following it continuously since leaving Persia several weeks prior, doesn't it seem odd that they would rejoice this strongly *When they saw the star*?

This rejoicing is inconsistent with a continuation of seeing what they had been already seeing. It supports a second appearing of the star. This second appearing of the star would certainly be a cause for rejoicing. It was a confirming sign to them. After weeks of 'blind' travel, we might expect they were beginning to wonder if they were imagining the star. If they hadn't had any further evidence of the birth of a king for weeks, probably months, then a second sign would have been cause indeed for rejoicing. I think this one short verse, Matthew 2:10, sends a clear message to us. In fact, this verse is what originally put me onto investigating this scenario in the first place. I had to wonder, 'Why did they rejoice?'

Behind-the-Scene

Another message of this story, when viewed in this light, is that on the basis of very little evidence the magi made a sacrificial effort to connect with spiritual reality. Although their understanding was clouded with idolatrous superstition and their motives were questionable, they came.

Of even more significance is that they were coming because God was calling to them. Amazingly He was calling to them on their terms.

We have in this passage unmistakable evidence that this was no ordinary star. It was sent from God. When they received God's clear sign, they rejoiced greatly. Is that not the beginning of true worship? They left Persia with the intent to pay homage to a future foreign king. That was their initial objective, I believe. They left Palestine having been contacted by the God Almighty of Israel, and I believe they now had a new definition of worship. They had a message to report to their people that was much greater than the one with which they began their travels. They began a journey but completed a quest. They started with homage but returned from a pilgrimage. They believed!

The Star, a Finale
This story seems to put to rest any naturalistic approach at explaining the star. At its first sighting while the magi were still in the East, we have no record of the star's behavior. In this second sighting, we have a good description of its very unique behavior. It had appeared while they were in the East, then vanished, and now reappeared. There is nothing natural or normal about that. In this last appearance of it, we see a characteristic that is unlike any natural star, planet, or comet. It did not remain stationary with respect to the other stars. Rather it moved ahead of them, came to rest, and somehow directed them to the precise location they were seeking. If the magi had not had a second look at the star, they would have continued on as directed by Herod to Bethlehem, and come up unsuccessful.

The scripture says, . . . *and behold, the star which they had seen in the East went before them, till it came and stood over where the young Child was.* How did they recognize that it was the same star they had seen in the East? We are not told how they knew. We are not told if it had an unusual appearance, perhaps a unique color or brightness. I believe they recognized it because of its characteristic abnormal movement. It is logical to assume that in its Persian sighting it also did not move with the other stars, but moved independently, as in the second sighting, and that this characteristic is what identified it as the star they had seen while still in the East. Certainly, its movement in this journey to Nazareth was unconventional. This star was specially-created for this one purpose—to herald the way to Jesus for the magi. It was no obstacle for the One who in an instant created all the lights in the universe, to create a special star and then remove it at His will. Based on the rendering of scripture, it is unreasonable to try to naturalize it. Even further, once we read carefully the characteristics of the star in scripture, continuing to pursue a naturalistic cause for it signals a denial of the validity of the scripture narrative.

Chapter 7

The Magi Worship

Matthew 2:11 (NKJV)
¹¹ And when they had come into the house, they saw the young Child with Mary His mother, and fell down and worshiped Him. And when they had opened their treasures, they presented gifts to Him: gold, frankincense, and myrrh.

<u>Their Humility</u>
Since the magi were now being led by the star, does this imply their arrival was at night? Jesus is no longer in the stable. He has long since moved into a house in Nazareth. Only the child Jesus and Mary are mentioned as being present. Was Joseph not present or just not mentioned? I think the latter. This large Persian entourage of obvious nobility arriving at a humble home in a small village, not on a main trade route, would certainly have drawn attention. More-so if their arrival was at night. Whatever the circumstance, they arrived to find Jesus, and no doubt the neighbors were buzzing.

When the magi saw the child, they fell down and worshipped. The word used for their posture signals not just a polite curtsy, nor even a deep bow. It describes that they fell prostrate, their faces to the ground, before the child. We might question the acceptability of their worship before God. After all, they are pagan astrologers. What would they know about true worship? However, as we have already said, it was God Himself who called the magi to this place. Whatever their motives and purposes were when they left Persia, there can be little doubt that they realized the call of the God of Israel and were worshipping from spiritually awakened hearts. They must have had a birth of faith in the God of Israel. I believe the Lord God accepted their worship of His Son that day.

Their Gifts
Their gifts were valuable items that would be compact and suitable for caravan travel. All three of the gifts mentioned might be seen as feasible elements of barter if they were on a business trip. They were a practical way of condensing wealth for travel. Remember too that these magi were originally making an international gesture, expecting that their gifts would be presented in the king's palace in Jerusalem. Thus, they were probably fairly substantial in value. Were they more than just random gifts of value?

Is it possible that after studying the prophecies about Messiah from the Hebrew scriptures, the magi purposefully chose gifts appropriate for the roles they discovered of him? Or is it likely that the gifts were selected with divine providential guidance unknown to them? Or were they just nice, valuable, appropriate gifts to bring, signifying nothing? We easily assume that gold was brought as being suitable for a king. Is it not reasonable, after studying the messianic prophecies, to assume the same intentional appropriateness for the other gifts?

Certainly, the gifts had value, and probably were sold by Joseph to sustain his small pilgrim family through the journey to Egypt that lay ahead. But the gospel writer Matthew thought it important to name these three gifts specifically. Thus, like so many others, I am inclined to look for figurative significance in them. It seems, at least, plausible speculation to assume the wise men were wise to such significance. What messages about Jesus are embodied in the gold, frankincense, and myrrh?

Gold – the Mark of Royalty
The Old Testament prophecies are replete with references to the kingship of this One who was to come, and we have already looked at several. I will just repeat this one example that we have already considered.

> *Daniel 7:13-14 (ESV)*
> [13] *"I saw in the night visions, and behold, with the clouds of heaven there came one like a son of man, and he came to the Ancient of Days and was presented before him.* [14] *And to him was given dominion and glory and a kingdom, that all peoples, nations, and languages should serve him; his dominion is an everlasting dominion, which shall not pass away, and his kingdom one that shall not be destroyed.*

Gold was an appropriate gift to give a king. It was the most valuable of metals known in ancient times. By bringing it, they were recognizing Jesus as a king, a very noteworthy king. We are told in Revelation that he is the *King of kings*.

Do we approach him as a king, albeit, a benevolent king? We do, if we rightly understand the title *Lord*. To approach him in any other way is unbiblical, as witnessed by the many who came to him for healing and called to him as *Lord*. Kings have dominion. As Christians, we are in his dominion. Do we have strongholds in our lives over which Jesus does not have dominion? The answer is yes, so long as we live in this present world. A sanctified life is one which is constantly finding and rooting out such exclusions to his Lordship. The recognition of this rightful Lordship is essential to salvation itself. The implementation of it is a life-long process.

> *Matthew 7:21 (ESV)*
> [21] *"Not everyone who says to me, 'Lord, Lord,' will enter the kingdom of heaven, but the one who does the will of my Father who is in heaven.*

Talk is cheap, but our behavior over time reveals our hearts. Entering the kingdom is all about being loyal subjects of the King. Gold reminds us of that royal status of Jesus in our lives. Our relationship with Jesus is described using many relational metaphors in scripture: shepherd-sheep, Father-children, husband-wife. This passage reminds us that our most foundational relationship must be as king-subject.

Frankincense – Emblem of Priesthood

Less prevalent in the Old Testament is the message of Messiah's role as high priest. This prophecy with messianic overtones was given to the prophet Zechariah.

Zechariah 6:12-13 (ESV)
[12] And say to him, 'Thus says the LORD of hosts, "Behold, the man whose name is the Branch: for he shall branch out from his place, and he shall build the temple of the LORD. [13] It is he who shall build the temple of the LORD and shall bear royal honor, and shall sit and rule on his throne. And there shall be a priest on his throne, and the counsel of peace shall be between them both."'

In New Testament teaching we more readily recognize Jesus as our high priest who sits at the Father's right hand as our advocate.

Hebrews 6:19-20 (ESV)
[19] We have this as a sure and steadfast anchor of the soul, a hope that enters into the inner place behind the curtain, [20] where Jesus has gone as a forerunner on our behalf, having become a high priest forever after the order of Melchizedek.

Hebrews 7:15-17 (ESV)
[15] This becomes even more evident when another priest arises in the likeness of Melchizedek, [16] who has become a priest, not on the basis of a legal requirement concerning bodily descent, but by the power of an indestructible life. [17] For it is witnessed of him, "You are a priest forever, after the order of Melchizedek."

Hebrews 8:1 (ESV)
[1] Now the point in what we are saying is this: we have such a high priest, one who is seated at the right hand of the throne of the Majesty in heaven,

Romans 8:34 (ESV)
³⁴ Who is to condemn? Christ Jesus is the one who died—more than that, who was raised—who is at the right hand of God, who indeed is interceding for us.

Frankincense reminds us of our security in Christ Jesus, our *anchor for the soul*, which depends on his adequacy as high priest, not on our performance in keeping the law. It is also emblematic of our Father-child relationship with God. Incense is used in scripture in symbolic fashion to represent the prayers of the saints being received by Him as a sweet aroma. God savors our prayerful interchange with Him. Our security rests on our loving relationship with him.

Ephesians 2:18-19 (ESV)
¹⁸ For through him we both have access in one Spirit to the Father. ¹⁹ So then you are no longer strangers and aliens, but you are fellow citizens with the saints and members of the household of God,

Myrrh – a Burial Balm

Myrrh was a strong perfume used to prepare a body for burial. It was quite expensive. John's gospel reports that Nicodemus and Joseph of Arimathea wrapped Jesus' body in linen strips, layered with seventy-five pounds of a mixture of myrrh and aloe, according to Jewish burial custom. This doesn't seem like a gift to bring a young child. Imagine yourself attending a baby shower or birth celebration and bringing a gift symbolic of death. This was not a gift of celebration. If there was symbolic meaning in this gift, it wasn't one of joyful congratulations.

The implication of it may not have been a complete surprise to Mary. She had heard the prophetic testimony of Simeon in the Jerusalem temple, saying:

Luke 2:34-35 (ESV)
³⁴ . . . "Behold, this child is appointed for the fall and rising of many in Israel, and for a sign that is opposed ³⁵ (and a sword

will pierce through your own soul also), so that thoughts from many hearts may be revealed."

From our perspective, we understand that in this prophecy a reference to the cross is in view. When John the Baptist first saw Jesus, he exclaimed, *Behold the Lamb of God who takes away the sins of the world,* envisioning a sacrificial lamb. When John the apostle turned to see the Lion of the tribe of Judah in Revelation 6, he saw instead *a lamb looking as if it had been slain.* Jesus gave *his life a ransom for many.* Jesus was born on earth to become a sacrificial lamb to atone for our sins. The shadow of the cross already stretched across that obscure birth, now back in Nazareth. This myrrh reminds us of that destiny.

> *Revelation 13:8 (ESV)*
> [8] *. . . written before the foundation of the world in the book of life of the Lamb who was slain.*

It might well have signaled a worrisome anticipation in Mary and Joseph too. For us, it is a symbol that brings hope and joy. When an Old Testament priest entered the tabernacle to atone for sins, he did not come empty-handed. He came bearing an acceptable sacrifice. When Jesus ascended into heaven, he too did not come empty-handed.

> *Hebrews 9:11-12 (ESV)*
> [11] *But when Christ appeared as a high priest of the good things that have come, then through the greater and more perfect tent (not made with hands, that is, not of this creation)* [12] *he entered once for all into the holy places, not by means of the blood of goats and calves but by means of his own blood, thus securing an eternal redemption.*

Just as Jesus' high priesthood is fully adequate for him to be our advocate, so also is his sacrificial death fully sufficient to cover our sins. Myrrh reminds us that we stand fully clothed in the righteousness of Christ before our Creator.

I don't know for sure if the magi knew these significances in the gifts, but we do understand them. Each Christmas when this story is read or performed, may the gold, frankincense, and myrrh henceforth be a standing reminder of the cost and sufficiency of our salvation. May they also remind us that this salvation is our Christmas gift from God.

A Principle of True Worship

None of us are worthy to approach God and be accepted. Yet He is there, ready to connect with us in our feeble attempts at worship. We come on the basis of His grace alone. The wise men *fell down* in their worship. They humbled themselves before this little child. Humility is a key ingredient in worship. Yes, it is appropriate for us to come boldly into the throne room of grace because of our confidence in the atoning blood of Christ. However, boldness is not brashness. Furthermore, boldness is not the opposite of humility. We will do well to learn from these magi how to approach God. They came humbly, recognizing their inferiority before him. Our confidence must spring from realizing God's merciful acceptance. This passage reminds us that humility is key to worship, whether we are a seeker or a veteran in the faith.

Chapter 8
Reflecting

What have we done in rocking some traditions surrounding the wise men? Is it just an academic exercise? Have we advanced our faith at all? This book is not written to simply criticize. I believe there are lessons we learn by clarifying truth. If we must unravel biblical fact or implied truth from tradition to make that happen, so be it.

First, let me say that in so doing, we have not removed the mystique of this narrative at all. On the contrary, the truth is still full of intrigue, and of the unexplained. In fact, I believe that intrigue is enhanced over the version clouded by tradition, but the intrigue is shifted from the mysterious unknown of the magi to the transcendent unsearchableness of God. When truth is blurred, the story--any story--can begin to take on the air of a fairy tale. In a more biblically accurate understanding, we see God acting not only through the miraculous but also through the providential. This latter aspect is more veiled in the traditional view.

What takeaways do we discover from this story when viewed more accurately? In this closing chapter we will briefly review some points already discussed and needing clarification. We will also recognize some general life principles that can be drawn from this story of the magi.

<u>Star Appearance</u>
We have proposed that the star was perhaps not noticed by anyone but the magi. If so, it was a sign to them, and not to anyone else in that day. We likewise suggest there is no biblical reason to assume the star was phenomenally bright. We suggest further that the star only appeared for a short while at the time of Jesus' birth. Then it disappeared and was not seen during the travels of the magi to Jerusalem. Finally, it reappeared to guide the magi on their trip from

Jerusalem to Nazareth. While it shone, it displayed very unique characteristics recognized by the magi. We suggest that the only stated such characteristic is that it moved independently, not traversing from east to west like the rest of the stars, but moving with independent purpose, leading them to the very house where Jesus was living. Its purpose fulfilled, we assume it disappeared once-and-for-all. In this scenario, the magi were not 'following' the star, until that last leg of the journey. This introduces the suggestion of a whole new vista of faith for these magi.

Away with Naturalism
Any attempt to explain the star that the magi saw using natural phenomenon is to completely ignore the scripture. No natural collusion of heavenly bodies could behave as this star is reported to have done. Trying to explain this star as a natural heavenly entity either ignores or denies the scripture, and leads to absurdity. This star can only be understood as a miraculous phenomenon. It appears that naturalism is absolutely inconsistent with the biblical account. To choose naturalism is to reject scripture.

In a more general sense, this argument reminds us that we must beware of seeking pragmatic solutions to spiritual issues.

Ephesians 6:12 (ESV)
[12] For we do not wrestle against flesh and blood, but against the rulers, against the authorities, against the cosmic powers over this present darkness, against the spiritual forces of evil in the heavenly places.

We in the western world, especially, tend to focus on what we can see, detect and measure. We are essentially blind to the larger spiritual strongholds around us. We only understand something of them from scripture. We must rely on God to guide us through the minefields of everyday living and to protect us from the unseen that surrounds us. That dependency is recognized and addressed in prayer. Prayer is our first battleground in the unseen world. Let us not become a victim of circumstance, blindsided by life. Become a prayer warrior as portrayed for us in the broader text of Ephesians 6.

The Awakening of the Magi

God's calling to the magi is unmistakable. Notice the ways in which He spoke to them. Consider the 'voices' He used. First, he spoke to them in perhaps the only way they could initially perceive. He gave them a star. From the prophecy of Balaam, we see that God planned this invasion of their world centuries before. Speaking to their superstitious minds, He spoke a message that would seem to make little sense to the Jews but spoke loudly and clearly to the magi. This message may have been specific for them.

Second, God spoke to the magi through Hebrew Prophecy. Just as they were prepared to *search diligently* to find the child, this new King of the Jews, they also likely did a lot of diligent collective research in Jewish scripture before setting out on such an arduous and monumental trip. They likely had available and may have employed a large number of researchers. As they read the prophecies, God spoke to them in the same way he speaks to us today through those same scriptures. As they began to see a big picture, their journey became something more; it likely became a pilgrimage.

Third, the Lord spoke to them through the mouths of the Jewish priests and scribes. As they heard these prophecy 'experts' confirm their purpose by giving them the exact birthplace from deep within the prophetic passages, God was affirming their mission. I think their anticipation was aroused by these words. At this time, they may have begun to be revitalized, encouraged that their pilgrimage was a valid endeavor. We might go so far as to say that at this point perhaps they began to see their journey as ordained, albeit by a God not their own. Was God in the process of calling them to be his own?

Fourthly, God spoke to them in the second appearance of the star that became their final guide. If the magi had any doubts, they were erased at this point. As a result, they were overjoyed. If our assumptions are accurate, then their joy would be expected. This second appearing of the star was much more than just a help to them finding their way. It was a confirming sign. The star didn't behave like other stars, but independently, as with purpose. They had to assign divine origin and purpose to it. They obviously saw it as a sign.

Fifth, God spoke to the magi by giving them success. They reached the goal of their pilgrimage. They found the child, the one destined in prophecy to be the king of an everlasting kingdom. The humble circumstances of his situation were not what they expected; not a palace as he would deserve, but because of all the voices they had heard, they did not question his authenticity. No mention is given of any extensive attempt to confirm he was the object of their search. The star was all they needed at this point. When they found him, they worshipped him. They immediately saw young Jesus as the goal of their journey. They immediately realized success and fulfillment of purpose.

Finally, the magi heard the voice of God in a dream. He warned them not to report back to Herod. This may have been their first sense of Herod's treachery. Until the dream, they seem oblivious to his plotting. They seem completely naïve in this matter. They appear to assume Herod's good will toward the new king. In addition to the dream's message changing their plans of return, it had to also impact their understanding of the God of Israel. They had to now see Him as a God of purpose and means. As they outwardly worshiped Jesus, they must have been worshipping God Almighty in their minds and wondering at his greatness. None of their idols had ever interacted with them in these ways. Any attempt to scrutinize their level of faith on the basis of this passage would be, at best, informed speculation. However, it is difficult to not see the repeated call of God to them and to behold a progressive awakening of the minds of these men. At the very least, we have to think that a foundation was laid for a possible future acceptance of the Messiah by those who would hear their story.

Satanic Agenda

The Bible is God's story of redemption for wayward man. From the beginning, a resistance has existed to God's redemptive purpose and plan. Satan has been working tirelessly to destroy that plan at every opportunity. In the Old Testament, his objective was to destroy the messianic lineage. He came close on many occasions, but God always brought rescue. The original lineage was broken when Cain killed Abel, but God raised up a new lineage in Seth. Satan tried to kill David by the hand of Saul, but God saved him out of Saul's hand. Satan enticed Athaliah to destroy David's whole family, but Joash was stolen away and saved while many of the other princes were murdered. While in exile in Persia, Satan engineered a plot to destroy all Jews under the edict of the king. The story of Esther tells of God's providential rescue from Jewish annihilation. Of course, the ultimate divine reversal of events occurred when Satan motivated evil leaders to crucify Jesus, only to find that he had served God's redemptive process and further sealed his own doom.

The story of God's rescue of baby Jesus from the hand of Herod is yet another in this litany of God's saving of the messianic line, and of Messiah himself. We often cannot see how our circumstances fit into the grand picture of redemption while we are in the trenches of everyday life. This serves as a reminder that we constantly need to lean on the Lord. We need him to be sovereign in our lives, not ourselves. We should pray constantly for God's providential protection and guidance for ourselves and our families, and for others because Satan's attacks continue in our lives today.

Our More Magnanimous God

In our traditional understanding of this story, we tend to see the magi as a peculiar group of strangers who wandered into the Christmas story, led by their curiosity. They departed with curiosity partially satisfied. I think when we strip away the traditions, and contemplate the reality of what likely happened based on scripture, we observe something wonderful about God. We see God making his salvation known to a people who were far away, not only geographically, but even more importantly--spiritually. We are reminded vividly that God condescended to not only become flesh and dwell among his chosen people, the Jews, but also to embrace the nations who are added to his 'chosen' list. This was envisioned in the Old Testament, and is expressed in the following prophetic verses.

Genesis 12:1-3 (ESV)
[1] Now the LORD said to Abram, "Go from your country and your kindred and your father's house to the land that I will show you. [2] And I will make of you a great nation, and I will bless you and make your name great, so that you will be a blessing. [3] I will bless those who bless you, and him who dishonors you I will curse, and in you all the families of the earth shall be blessed."

Psalm 22:27 (ESV)
[27] All the ends of the earth shall remember and turn to the LORD, and all the families of the nations shall worship before you.

Psalm 57:9-11 (ESV)
[9] I will give thanks to you, O Lord, among the peoples; I will sing praises to you among the nations. [10] For your steadfast love is great to the heavens, your faithfulness to the clouds. [11] Be exalted, O God, above the heavens! Let your glory be over all the earth!

Psalm 67:4-5 (ESV)
[4] Let the nations be glad and sing for joy, for you judge the peoples with equity and guide the nations upon earth. Selah [5] Let the peoples praise you, O God; let all the peoples praise you!

Isaiah 49:6 (ESV)
[6] he says: "It is too light a thing that you should be my servant to raise up the tribes of Jacob and to bring back the preserved of Israel; I will make you as a light for the nations, that my salvation may reach to the end of the earth."

God's redemptive plan was much more ambitious than the average first-century Jew understood or wanted to consider. It was his plan to 'graft in' the people of the nations of the earth who would believe—to graft them into the Kingdom of Heaven. That was the reason Jesus' return didn't occur immediately after his resurrection. It was delayed, and is still delayed, so that the *whole number of Gentiles* can come in. Then he will return to bring salvation to his children who are eagerly anticipating his appearing. Praise God for His loving, seeking heart!

Not only do we see God's great ambition and purpose, but we see his unimaginable condescension. Consider the gulf he spanned in calling to the magi. God had called out for Himself a nation descending from Abraham, separating them from the idolatry of the eastern cultures. This new lineage would bring forth the Messiah. To the new nation, God gave many commands. The majority of them were in direct opposition to the idolatrous practices and character that Abraham was called to leave behind. All forms of the magical arts were strictly forbidden. Astrology was forbidden. Now consider that in the story of the magi He didn't just overlook those practices, but He actually worked through them to establish a relationship with the magi. His benevolent mercy extended to these people reflects his grace and mercy toward all people, even you and me. In this light, there is one other group to which the star is a sign. It is a sign to readers of Matthew's narrative. The star is signaling to you and to me.

God's grand purpose is to gather to himself a group of faithful worshippers from all the peoples of the earth. His purpose will ultimately be fulfilled. We find a preview of this in John's prophetic message.

> *Revelation 7:9-10 (ESV)*
> *[9] After this I looked, and behold, a great multitude that no one could number, from every nation, from all tribes and peoples and languages, standing before the throne and before the Lamb, clothed in white robes, with palm branches in their hands, [10] and*

crying out with a loud voice, "Salvation belongs to our God who sits on the throne, and to the Lamb!"

After his resurrection, Jesus gave his disciples this command:

> *Matthew 28:18-20 (ESV)*
> *[18] And Jesus came and said to them, "All authority in heaven and on earth has been given to me. [19] Go therefore and make disciples of all nations, baptizing them in the name of the Father and of the Son and of the Holy Spirit, [20] teaching them to observe all that I have commanded you. And behold, I am with you always, to the end of the age."*

Still later he told them:

> *Acts 1:8 (ESV)*
> *[8] But you will receive power when the Holy Spirit has come upon you, and you will be my witnesses in Jerusalem and in all Judea and Samaria, and to the end of the earth."*

The mission of Matthew 28:18-20 is the same as that for which groundwork was being laid in the call of the magi. Much earlier, it was foretold in the prophecies of Israel. Earlier still, its foundation was being laid in the prophecy of Balaam. All this so that they would come.

If God's command is to redeem worshippers from every nation, every people group, every age, then it should define our own great mission. The visit of the magi reminds us to constantly reset our cosmic priority for this mission. When the mission is completed, then the grand purpose will be fulfilled; to gather worshippers for Jesus from the whole world for all eternity. That is our reasonable and appropriate worship because He is worthy! And when worship is given to the Son, then the Father is glorified. This is God's purpose for the ages.

Made in the USA
Middletown, DE
02 November 2024